THE SERENGETI

LAND OF ENDLESS SPACE

THE SERENGETI
LAND OF ENDLESS SPACE

LISA AND SVEN-OLOF LINDBLAD

FOREWORD BY GEORGE B. SCHALLER

CONTRIBUTIONS BY ALLAN EARNSHAW,

SANDY PRICE, AND KEITH SHACKLETON

RIZZOLI
NEW YORK

We dedicate this book to the dream
that the integrity of that which is
beautiful yet fragile may endure.

Front cover: Giraffe under an umbrella tree
Back cover: Zebras on plain
Page 1: Bull elephant
Title page: Cheetah family

First published in the United States of America in 1989 by
RIZZOLI INTERNATIONAL PUBLICATIONS, INC.
300 Park Avenue South, New York, NY 10010

Copyright © 1989 Rizzoli International Publications, Inc.
and Special Expeditions

Library of Congress Cataloging-in-Publication Data

Serengeti, land of endless space / edited by Lisa and Sven-Olof
    Lindblad; foreword by George B. Schaller; with contributions by
    Allan Earnshaw, Keith Shackleton, and Sandy Price.
        ISBN 0-8478-1096-8   ISBN 0-8478-1097-6 (pbk.)
        1. Zoology—Tanzania—Serengeti Plain.   2. Natural history—
    Tanzania—Serengeti Plain.   3. Serengeti Plain (Tanzania)
    I. Lindblad, Lisa.   II. Lindblad, Sven-Olof.
QL337.T3S44   1989   89-4041
508.678'27—dc20   CIP

Design by Gilda Hannah
Map by Joe Le Monnier
Composition by David E. Seham Associates, Inc.
Printed and bound in Italy

CONTENTS

Map   7

FOREWORD   9
George B. Schaller

ASH, RAIN, EARTH, FIRE   21
Allan Earnshaw

CYCLED RHYTHMS   57
Keith Shackleton

PRESERVING THE SERENGETI   109
Sandy Price

SIRENKET   147
Lisa Lindblad

Select Bibliography   175

About the Contributors   176

Photograph Credits   176

ACKNOWLEDGMENTS

We are grateful for the help we have received from many people. David Babu, Director of Tanzania's National Parks, was supportive of the book project from the beginning. Allan and Moira Earnshaw, John and Angela Sutton, Aadje Geertsma, and Everest Buganga were invaluable friends, offering inexhaustible support in East Africa. Closer to home, we must thank Andrew Jaffe for reading portions of the manuscript and Jerry Kuehner from Lexington Camera. At Rizzoli, we have had the guidance of, by now old friends, our editor Solveig Williams, our designer Gilda Hannah, and Howard Reeves. To everyone, our thanks.

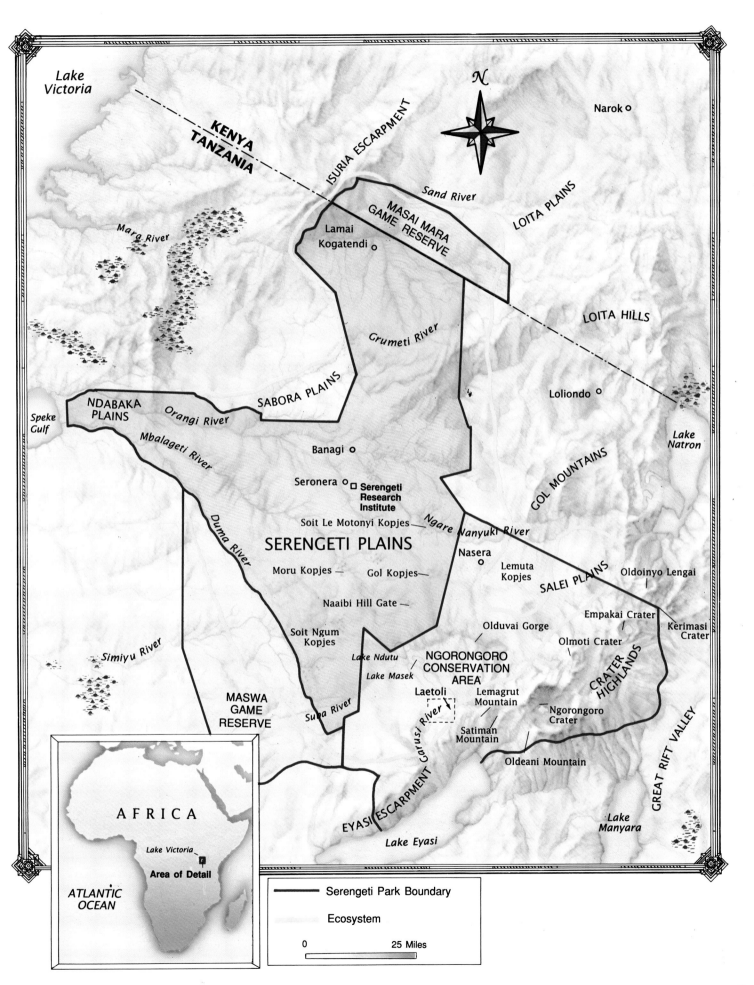

Lake Victoria

KENYA
TANZANIA

ISURIA ESCARPMENT

Sand River

Narok o

LOITA PLAINS

Mara River

MASAI MARA GAME RESERVE

Lamai Kogatendi o

LOITA HILLS

Grumeti River

Loliondo o

SABORA PLAINS

Speke Gulf

NDABAKA PLAINS

Orangi River

Mbalageti River

Lake Natron

GOL MOUNTAINS

Banagi o

Seronera o □ Serengeti Research Institute

Soit Le Motonyi Kopjes —

Ngare Nanyuki River

SERENGETI PLAINS

Duma River

Nasera o

Lemuta Kopjes

SALEI PLAINS

Oldoinyo Lengai

Moru Kopjes —

Gol Kopjes —

Naaibi Hill Gate —

Empakai Crater

Kerimasi Crater

Olduvai Gorge

Olmoti Crater

Soit Ngum Kopjes

Simiyu River

Lake Ndutu

Lake Masek

NGORONGORO CONSERVATION AREA

Laetoli

Lemagrut Mountain

CRATER HIGHLANDS

Ngorongoro Crater

MASWA GAME RESERVE

Suba River

Satiman Mountain

Oldeani Mountain

EYASI ESCARPMENT

Garusi River

Lake Manyara

GREAT RIFT VALLEY

Lake Eyasi

AFRICA

Lake Victoria

Area of Detail

ATLANTIC OCEAN

— Serengeti Park Boundary

···· Ecosystem

0   25 Miles

FOREWORD

The survival of our wildlife is a matter of grave concern to all of us in Africa. These wild creatures amid the wild places they inhabit are not only important as a source of wonder and inspiration but are an integral part of our national resources and of our future livelihood and well-being.

Julius Kambarage Nyerere,
former President of Tanzania

For over three years during the late 1960s my wife Kay, two small sons, and I made our home in the Serengeti National Park. We lived in a wooden bungalow shaded by flat-topped acacias where plains gave way to woodlands at a place called Seronera. Daily I roamed in search of lions whose life I had come to study. At the beginning of the dry season in May when grass on the plains becomes dry stubble and the sky is cloudless and pale as if seen through a luminous gauze, much of the wildlife retreats to the woodlands where grass and water are plentiful. Wildebeest and zebra flow westward, a throbbing stream of life drawn by a collective will, the animals trudging in long lines, often several abreast. They follow their age-old migration west and then north, many moving out of Tanzania into Kenya's Masai Mara Game Reserve.

I liked the woodlands in spite of persistent tsetse flies. Lemon-barked fever trees line stream banks and borassus palms are there too in primitive elegance. Herds of skittish impala come to drink at pools, elephants move like floating gray boulders through the thickets, and flocks of Fisher's lovebirds pass overhead, handfuls of emeralds tossed into the sky. When in November or December black pillars of rain announce a change of season, the migratory animals return to the plains to feast on nutrient-rich grass. It pleased me to follow this vagrant wandering—I liked the plains best.

Nomadic lions trailed the great herds too, and resident prides at the edge of the woodlands shifted into the open. I watched them in daytime, the animals conveying indolent power even when in repose. I followed them also on hunts at night, the plains suffused with the moon's silver light. The

Pages 8–9: Elephant herd in the Masai Mara Game Reserve

Pages 10–11: Lioness basking on the Gol Kopjes

thunder of fleeing herds shattered the silence, and sometimes the dying scream of a zebra. The cats bolted down the meat snarling and snapping, their emotions so naked that the scene filled me with primal fear even in the safety of a Land Rover. The air was heavy with the odor of blood and rumen content.

Sometimes, however, I abandoned this scientific quest to venture onto plains where there were no roads, no people, nothing to violate the peace, where there were only animals and the green curve of a horizon broken by wind-worn outcrops of stone called kopjes. There wildebeest croaked like gigantic frogs, Thompson's gazelles twitched their tails, and vultures soared stiff-winged overhead. It was a scene of pastoral delight, of an eternal beginning where animals lived unaffected by today's complexities. I left my vehicle behind and, deprived of this armor, strode across the sea of grass, a lone figure free to roam, intoxicated by the wild beauty and vastness that humankind has not yet shaped to its will. I climbed a kopje, eyed by blue-and-red agama lizards, and reclined on the warm rock, exposed to, yet converging with, the environment.

Below, in brilliant light, heat waves danced like a choppy sea before the wind and distorted wildebeest, zebra, eland and others into phantom creatures. Ancient connections seemingly at the edge of memory crowded the mind, and dreams of resurrecting the past were almost palpable. Over a million years ago this landscape with its acacia woodlands, plains, and lakes was much as it is today, but the fauna was much more diverse, a biologist's delight. Around and on my kopje roamed various species now extinct for reasons unknown. Chalicotheres, related to horses and tapirs, moved by ponderously; a giraffe with palmate horns, *Libytherium*, browsed on trees; *Simopithecus*, gorilla-sized baboons, scampered over the kopje; *Afrochoerus*, a long-tusked pig as large as a rhinoceros, rooted in nearby swamps; and saber-toothed cats prowled the shadows. To the east, near the base of the highlands, lies Olduvai Gorge, where humankind had its roots, a vanished legacy of various hominids. They, too, sat on this kopje. But unlike them, I bore witness to the last days of Eden, the last great gathering of herds; I saw no more than a fragile illusion of the Pleistocene.

Since the 1950s many biologists have worked in the Serengeti ecosystem, an area of 10,000 square miles. The Serengeti Research Institute was established in 1966 and continues under the name of Serengeti Wildlife Research Center with Karim Hirji its current Tanzanian director. Research on animals, vegetation, climate, soils and other topics has contributed to an understanding of how the ecosystem works. In 1957, Bernhard and Michael Grzimek were pioneers whose book *Serengeti Shall Not Die* focused the world's consciousness on that priceless heritage hidden in Tanzania. A. R. E. Sinclair has devoted over two decades to monitoring populations of wildebeest, buffalo, and other species, and Sam McNaughton has studied the interactions between grasses and herbivores for many years, to mention two individuals whose long-term efforts have made important contributions towards protecting and managing the Serengeti. In the Ngorongoro Conservation Unit adjoining the Serengeti, Patricia Moehlman trains teams of Tanzanians in ecological monitoring techniques. This essential task has too long been neglected by expatriate researchers, even though the future of the Serengeti depends on the initiative, dedication, and knowledge of Tanzanians.

The Serengeti has a long past but a brief history, written records dating back only to the turn of the century. Yet even this brief span serves as a reminder that the Serengeti as we know it is but a fragile moment in time, that no ecosystem remains static. Rinderpest, a viral disease whose natural host is cattle, struck East Africa in 1890 and within two years about ninety-five percent of the wildebeest and buffalo had died. Deprived of life-sustaining livestock, many Masai and other tribesmen perished in famine; deprived of wildlife, some lions became man-eaters. People retreated from the Serengeti region, their departure reducing woodland fires which had kept growth in check by killing seedlings. Grass glades now converted to thickets. Veterinary treatment of livestock eliminated the disease in cattle and by the early 1960s it had disappeared in the wildlife as well. Wildebeest and buffalo now increased rapidly in number. Wildebeest rose from 250,000 in 1961 to 500,000 in 1967, and buffalo from 30,000 to 50,000 during the same period, whereas zebra, not affected by the disease, remained stable in number.

Page 13: Sausage tree

Pages 14–15: Migrating zebras and wildebeest in the Masai Mara Game Reserve

A new factor began to have an impact on the wildlife in 1971. Lack of rainfall during the dry season had limited the grass supply of herbivores, keeping populations in check, but suddenly more frequent and widespread showers enabled some populations to expand to new limits. Wildebeest reached 1.3 million by 1977, then leveled off; buffalo increased to 75,000, and topi also became more abundant. As settlers arrived in ever larger numbers around the periphery of the park, fires progressively turned woodland to grassland. But now with so many wildebeest eating and trampling the tall grass, the incidence of fire declined, allowing greater regeneration of trees. The country became more bushy, as in the early part of this century, benefiting browsers such as the giraffe. Today with more grass available on the plains during the dry season, gazelle, zebra and others remain there in greater numbers, which, in turn, has enabled hyenas to increase. New lion prides have established themselves where none could exist before and those already present increased in size. A climatic change back to the drier period may well cause the wildebeest population to crash and once more initiate far-reaching changes in the ecosystem.

Poachers also have an impact on wildlife. In the mid-1970s lack of funds almost halted anti-poaching efforts for a decade. Buffalo were reduced by more than fifty percent and elephants, who greatly effect woodlands by pushing over mature trees, by eighty-five percent, reducing the herd to a mere 350 animals.

The web of life is intricate, the relationships complex. Much of the research in the Serengeti has a significant application when making decisions about the ecosystem's future. At present the integrity of the park is threatened by encroaching agriculturalists, poachers, a railroad, and cattle ranches. And someone has actually proposed that "the Serengeti migration could produce perhaps forty million tins of canned meat each year without any decline in the total wildebeest, zebra, and gazelle numbers. . . ." Other considerations aside, cropping wildlife would promote instability in the ecosystem, upsetting the dynamic balance between herbivores and their food supply and between predator and prey. And it would negate three decades of research on the natural regulation of animal numbers.

Forty million tins of canned meat. Preservation for profit should not be the ultimate goal. Tanzania has maintained the Serengeti in spite of crushing social needs not for economic reasons but as a statement of the nation's vision and identity. The Serengeti does, however, have inestimable value as a genetic storehouse of numerous species. At some future date, when we are ready to mend and restore what this century has squandered, the grasses and animals may provide stock for rehabilitating other pastures. Parks such as the Serengeti also provide valuable natural laboratories, baselines against which changes elsewhere can be measured and placed into perspective. But, above all, certain places are so unique in the pleasure and inspiration they afford that they must be preserved without compromise as repositories of beauty—as living museums. They must remain unmanaged as original fragments of our past. Unaffected by human greed, their survival will be witness to man's moral obligation to society and to other species. And there must be a global commitment to maintain such cultural resources. As Edward Hoagland phrased it in another context, the Serengeti should be viewed as "the best and final future place to make a leisurely traverse or enjoy a camping trip that was not rooted in our century."

Yearning for hope and thriving on dreams, we find what we seek in Serengeti. At least once in a lifetime every person should make a pilgrimage into the wilderness to dwell on its wonders and discover the idyll of a past now largely gone. If I had to select just one such spot on earth, it would be the Serengeti. There dwell the fierce ghosts of our human past, there animals seek their destiny, living monuments to a time when we were still wanderers on a prehistoric earth. To witness that calm rhythm of life revives our worn souls and recaptures a feeling of belonging to the natural world. No one can return from the Serengeti unchanged, for tawny lions will forever prowl our memory and great herds throng our imagination.

GEORGE B. SCHALLER
Wildlife Conservation International

Page 17: Klipspringers
Pages 18–19: Hippo pool in the Mara River

ASH, RAIN, EARTH, FIRE

On a late November morning, under a lowering sky that threatened rain, the ancient volcano Satiman began to erupt as it had done many times in the past. Several times its rumbles shook the earth as successive clouds of ash were coughed up to be gently carried out across the plains on a quickening easterly breeze. Low rolls of thunder preceded the shower of light rain that began to fall over the still-warm ashes.

It was the beginning of the rainy season, that is if the rains were to continue. No two years were the same, and sometimes the rains never came, or they were late, or they petered out early. The wind wailed dolefully through the pierced galls of the stunted whistling-thorn acacia that dotted these southeastern expanses of vast, endless savannah that would some day be called the Serengeti Plains. Guinea fowl scolded as they scuttled over the gray dust, and baboon mothers moaned gently as they searched for protected areas where the grasses had not as yet been covered by ashfall. A herd of elephants, leaving the volcano's forested foothills, repeatedly swung their heads from side to side, lifting their trunks to test the wind, trying to gauge the best direction to take. Three-toed horses were on the move, too. Only a giraffe seemed untroubled as it traipsed listlessly towards a line of distant trees.

The mood must even have affected the trio of erect, two-legged creatures who, only that morning, had set off in the direction of Lemuta. A tree-clad inselberg on the western side of the Gol Mountains, it was the perfect base for the wet season when the migratory herds of wildebeest, horses, and antelope returned to the short-grass plains. There would be plenty of dead animals to scavenge and many fewer hyenas and saber-toothed cats to contend with than in the woodlands. Nevertheless, it was a long jour-

Pages 20–21: Sunrise at Moru Kopjes

Pages 22–23: Wildflowers after the rains

ney, and they had been content to camp in the valley of the fig trees. And now Satiman had started to erupt again. At one point, the female half-turned, looking back, undecided. Then her mate beckoned her on, and they resumed their trudge northwards through the moist ash, one behind the other, the female putting her feet in the male's tracks, for the ash was still quite hot in places, her child striding independently to her left.

Poetic licence? A light-hearted fantasy? Yet a modern-day hunter, such as an individual of the Hadza tribe from nearby Lake Eyasi, would not have the slightest problem reconstructing this picture from a quick glance at the fossil footprints. Apart from the prints of a chalicothere, a strange, claw-footed ungulate, all the tracks look almost as if they might have been made only yesterday by animals still in existence. Samples of black mica, or biotite, taken from ash layers above and below the prints, however, yield an antiquity of 3.6 million years.

It is September of 1976 and we are with Dr. Mary Leakey and her associates at the end of her second season just south of the Serengeti at a place the Masai call Laetoli, in reference to the blood-red fireball lilies that erupt from the earth in profusion with the first rains. Dr. Leakey is here on a hunch that "the mystique of Laetoli had eluded us," referring to an earlier visit to the area with her late husband, Dr. Louis S. B. Leakey. She was right. In a totally unscientific manner, the fossil footprints have literally been stumbled upon by a visiting paleontologist, Dr. Andrew Hill, in his attempt to avoid a ball of elephant dung thrown at him by another visitor to Laetoli, ecologist Dr. David Western. In such mysterious ways does the search for knowledge sometimes take a step forward. It will take three more years to complete the dig and uncover all the footprints, but the momentous nature of the find is already apparent. In addition to the footprints, the fossilized bones of twenty-two individuals will also be uncovered. Together with the footprints, they indicate that the Laetoli hominids were less than five feet tall, lightly built, and small-brained. They appear to be very similar in type to later hominid specimens found in Ethiopia by Dr. Donald C. Johanson and named by him *Australopithecus afarensis,* and also to specimens found by Raymond Dart at Makapansgat in South Africa that are now thought to be approximately three million years old.

We next pick up the tracks of early man some thirty miles to the north of Laetoli and one and a half million years later, at the dawn of the Pleistocene era. The area is called by the Masai "Olduvai," meaning "the place of the wild sisal," and its paleontological significance was first recognized by a Professor Kattwinkel in 1911 while butterfly collecting. The Olduvai Gorge is a thirty-five mile long, Y-shaped valley on the southeastern plains of the Serengeti. It was cut by a fast-flowing river less than half a million years ago and, in the process, a layer cake of time was exposed. Fifty years of painstaking fieldwork by the Leakeys at Olduvai has yielded the most complete and continuous record of man's past found anywhere on earth.

Two million years ago there was no Olduvai Gorge. Instead, there was an ancient lake six miles by three miles that was formed during the creation of the Great Rift Valley. Between Laetoli and Olduvai a great deal of tectonic activity had taken place. Satiman had been joined by a string of other active volcanoes, all with lyrical names like Oldeani, Ngorongoro, Losirua, Lemagrut, and Empakai. Developing along a twenty-million-year-old fault line, these volcanoes had coalesced to form the Crater Highlands. Some of these volcanoes were much taller than they are today. Ngorongoro, for example, was probably 15,000 feet at the summit before it blew its top. Today, it is half that height, having collapsed internally to form a huge caldera whose one hundred square mile floor is one of the finest places to observe wildlife in the world. The mountain forest that mantled the slopes of these volcanoes covered an area two or three times larger than it does today, and numerous small rivers and streams coursed down their slopes. Simultaneously, a renewed phase of massive geological faulting created the Great Rift Valley, opening up a gigantic fracture line east of the volcanoes that runs from the Okavango Delta in the south of the continent to the Danakil Desert in the north, and then on into Eastern Europe. Lakes Manyara, Natron, Eyasi, and Olduvai were all created during this period as the streams and rivers tumbling down the slopes of the volcanoes or cascading down the craggy scarps of the Rift Wall emptied into landlocked basins.

The formation of the vast, virtually treeless grasslands so typical of the eastern and southern Serengeti plains also dates back to this era of intense volcanic

Page 25: Gong rocks, used as a musical instrument, at Moru Kopjes

Pages 26–27: Olduvai Gorge during the wet season

activity. Even before the eruption of Satiman in whose ash the Laetoli footprints were immortalized, volcanoes constantly vented their ashy grievances over the great plains. Even today, there is still one active volcano at the northern end of the Crater Highlands, Oldoinyo Lengai, whose ashfall in the 1940 eruption was carried as far as Seronera, sixty miles away. Wherever the winds have carried the ash there are treeless plains, the result of the peculiar structure of volcanic soils.

The soils closest to the volcanoes are made up of coarse, sandy particles that are too heavy to be taken far by the wind, while those farthest from the volcanoes are composed of the lighter and more finely textured ash. Where the soils are more porous, as in the sandier ash closest to the volcanoes, the bedrock is closer to the surface. The roots of trees, bushes, and even grasses are unable to penetrate this hardpan. Where the soil particles are finer, they are more moisture retentive, and the soil deeper and less salty, but still no trees can grow here. This east-west spectrum of variation in soil texture, moisture retentivity, and salt concentration is reflected in the varying height and luxuriance of the grasses, from the dwarf forms of drop-seed and star grasses of the short-grass Eastern Plains to the rich stands of red-oat and bamboo grass toward the margins of the western woodlands that, when the rains are true, grow as high as the backs of the grazing animals.

A study of fossil pollens at Olduvai has indicated that the climate there two million years ago was much wetter than it is today, with a rainfall of thirty-five inches a year instead of the current yearly average of thirty inches. Acacia woodland surrounded the lake and there may even have been some groundwater forest where the fresh-water streams came off the slopes of the volcanoes in a landscape very reminiscent of Lake Manyara today. Grasslands covered the plains and intervened between acacia woodland and forest, and the shoreline was lined with reeds and sedges that, in some areas, formed extensive marshes that flooded in the wet season.

A veritable treasure trove of fossil vertebrate remains paints a remarkable picture of the living inhabitants of this long-ago lakeshore environment. Crocodiles seem to have been common, thriving on catfish as well as animals coming to the lake to drink. Hippo were there, but not in large numbers, probably due to the alkalinity of the lake. Flamingoes, on the other hand, reveled in the alkaline conditions and their bones have even been found on the floors of early man, indicating that they were often on the menu. Gulls, terns, skimmers, grebes, cormorants, and pelicans all used the open waters of the lake, while the reed beds and marshes provided perfect cover for the storks, herons, rails and jacanas. These marshy areas were also the favorite haunt of reedbuck, kob, lechwe, and waterbuck and were visited by rhino, both black and white, in search of mud wallows. Elephant and giraffe are known to have frequented the acacia woodland and groundwater forest, while pigs and members of the horse family, including zebra, would have congregated on the grasslands near the lake and out on the plains.

Twenty living sites of early man dated between 1.8 and 1.6 million years ago have been found along the edge of the lake. Most of them are along the eastern margins where the streams and small rivers entering the lake would have provided year-round fresh water, shade, and plenty of game. Of these sites, the oldest stands out above the rest. Like the Laetoli footprints, it is a crucial marker in the story of man's evolution. Known as DK after Donald McInnes Korongo, the site's remains look as if they might once have formed a circle of lava boulders. A close look at the fossil debris within and without the circle reveals a fascinating pattern. Inside there is a concentration of limb bones that all show signs of having been smashed open to expose the marrow. Scattered among them are numerous lava flakes that would have been used to cut off the meat. Outside, however, are the remains of bones such as shoulderblades and jaws that do not contain marrow, together with a collection of heavier stone artifacts. One concludes the lava circle is more than just a windbreak but a place shared by a group of people over a period of time: somewhere that animal remains could be brought back to, butchered, and communally consumed, together with whatever fruits, berries, and roots had also been collected. It was, in fact, a home. DK is also special because of its stone tools which belong to the Oldowan culture. Simple though they are—mainly choppers and flakes—they are nevertheless among the oldest stone tools yet discovered. In the fifty square miles of deposits at Laetoli, not a single stone implement has been found. Man may have walked upright 3.6 million years ago, thereby freeing his hands for tool-

Page 29: Giraffes under Nasera Rock

Pages 30–31: Shifting sands in Ngorongoro Conservation Unit

making, but he did not seize this opportunity for another million and a half years.

Who constructed the circle of lava boulders? Who made these stone tools? Paleontologists do not know for sure but the available evidence points to *Homo habilis*, "handy man," the oldest hominid to be regarded as a member of the genus *Homo*. Another hominid, *Australopithecus boisei*, is also present on that ancient Olduvai shoreline, a contemporary of *Homo habilis*. *Boisei*, however, is not the same species as the trio that walked across the ash-covered plains at Laetoli, being far more robustly built and with jaws so massive that it popularly became known as "Nutcracker Man." Both *Australopithecus boisei* and *Homo habilis* are joined at Olduvai some 1.5 million years ago by a third hominid species called *Homo erectus*.

By the time of *Homo erectus*, major faulting had reduced the Olduvai lake to about a third of its former size. By 1.2 million years ago it had disappeared completely to be replaced by an alluvial plain dotted with pans and marshes, resembling the area around Lake Ndutu today. With the lake gone, the streams coming from the Crater Highlands had united into a single river flowing west into Lake Victoria. At first *Homo erectus* found an environment that, if anything, was wetter and lusher than ever before. Dense evergreen forest covered large areas, supporting a spectacular array of megafaunal species such as a baboon the size of a gorilla, a pig the size of a hippo, and an enormous relative of the buffalo with horn-spans exceeding eighty inches. Unfortunately for these giants, a dry phase followed this period, ultimately leading to their extinction as they competed for survival with better adapted species. This trend towards greater aridity was to continue into modern times, despite the occasional return to wetter conditions. Wildebeest, hartebeest, and topi begin to be found in great numbers in the fossil record, as do many gazelle species. This trend towards greater aridity, however, should not be overemphasized. The remarkable fact about the Serengeti's climate during the Pleistocene era is its stability. It has fluctuated within relatively narrow limits, maintaining its savannah character while other areas, such as the central Kenya highlands, became part of the vast equatorial forests of Zaire on at least two occasions during periods of higher rainfall. Seasonal climatic fluctuations did, however, become more pronounced for the next million years which, in all likelihood, means that the spectacular animal migrations one sees in the Serengeti today of herds moving from wet season to dry season pastures and back again have been taking place since then.

Into this hunter's cornucopia strides *Homo erectus*, destined to become the single most successful and dominant hominid in the landscape for virtually the next million and a half years. The key to the success of this creature is a superior stone tool kit, the development of which is so significant in the history of man's evolution that it ranks with the invention of the wheel and the sail. This stone technology centered around the manufacture and use of hand axes.

These stone tools carry the story of the later phases of human evolution in the Serengeti as, unfortunately, the fossil record at Olduvai and Laetoli from 400,000 years ago to the present is noticeably sparse and unrevealing. Microlithic stone tools in the Serengeti start from the Middle Stone Age, approximately 120,000 years ago, and are most commonly found in the vicinity of kopjes. These rock islands became the focus of activity for our early ancestors as a more transhumant lifestyle gradually came into being with the disappearance of permanent water sources on the plains and the advent of a drier climate marked by seasonal fluctuations. With no lake or permanent rivers, the plains would only have been used during the rainy season from November to May when the great migratory herds of animals returned from the north and west. In the dry season, from June to November, the hunter-gatherer bands would have moved back to the edge of the woodlands where resident species of game could be found and where rivers, such as the Simiyu, Seronera, Grumeti, and Mbalageti—permanent water sources—drained into Lake Victoria. With this transhumant existence, the kopjes became especially important. They provided vital catchment pools of rainwater as well as shade and shelter from the cold east winds. They also were unparalleled vantage points from which to scan for potential prey animals and perhaps even hostile intruders.

Granite islands in an ocean of grass, these kopjes were formed between 475 and 650 million years ago when the Serengeti was an ancient inland sea, a sea that filled a downwarp in the earth's crust at a time of gigantic convulsions deep in the core of the planet. Sand, mud, and shale brought by rivers formed

Page 33: Lion

Pages 34–35: Natural rock sculpture

multiple sedimentary layers, only to be folded inwards and then upwards to form a chain of mountains. Where these folded rocks appeared above the earth's surface, they were immediately subjected to the forces of erosion that, over the eons, have reduced them to the gentle undulating relief which is so characteristic of the Serengeti plains today. Deep in the roots of the mountain chain, however, tremendous heat and pressure metamorphosed the sedimentary rocks into molten granite that, in places, rose under pressure to the earth's surface, cooling and crystallizing on the way, to become kopjes. Nutritious soils, derived from the weathering of kopje granite, together with rain water held in catchment basins, have turned many of these ancient Precambrian rock outcrops into green oases, complete with trees, shrubs, and wildflowers, often to be found situated in otherwise treeless and waterless expanses of grassland.

Wherever they are situated, in grassland or woodland, each kopje complex has its own very distinct character. Gol Kopjes, for example, has a stark beauty, situated far out in the middle of an austere nowhere; while windy Lemuta Kopjes is reminiscent of a Japanese bonsai garden where not only the plants but even the rocks, themselves, appear to be perfectly scaled miniatures. The monolithic kopje of Nasera is the Serengeti's answer to Ayers Rock, and at Sametu it is as if the now extinct elephant bird of Madagascar had laid a clutch of giant stone eggs, their smooth grey granite as distinct as the colorful cinnamon and rose crenellations of Soit Ngum Kopjes. Some kopjes are lone citadels, like Nasera and Soit le Motonyi, while lyrical Moru Kopjes, the most extensive of these granite leviathans, covers an area of twenty-five square miles of glorious parkland. Unique as they are, they have one thing in common—mystique. It is the mystique of Stonehenge and the sarsens of Avebury. A mystique born of an association with great antiquity.

Digs at Nasera Rock on the easternmost margins of the Serengeti Plains and along the Loiyangalani stream just below Moru Kopjes have provided evidence of microlithic technology over 100,000 years old. In the case of Nasera, this evidence continues to be found in successive layers right up to the present, thereby providing a fascinating chronicle of those years. Both Nasera and Moru Kopjes guard the entrances to migratory corridors, through the Gol

Pages 36–37: Oldoinyo Lengai covered in soda ash after the 1967 eruption

Page 38: Barafu Kopjes

Page 39: Old-Man's-Beard lichen on trees on Ngorongoro Crater's rim

Mountains onto the Salei Plains in the case of Nasera, and through the Itonjo Hills to the Western Corridor in the case of Moru Kopjes. Hunting became increasingly important to *Homo sapiens*, now armed with the superior weapons of microlithic technology, and what better places to wait for the massing herds of wildebeest, zebra and gazelle than the granite monoliths of Nasera and Moru?

Hunting continued to play an important role in the lifestyle of our neolithic ancestors even after they had successfully introduced domesticated animals into their economy, an event which, in the Serengeti, occurred some three to five thousand years ago. These pioneers of the Pastoral Neolithic period in East Africa have been called the Stone Bowl people, so called because of the stone bowls they used in their daily lives. Culturally and linguistically they are classified as southern Cushites who migrated to the highland plains of the Serengeti from an area in that corner of the Horn of Africa where the Sudan, Kenya and Ethiopia come together. They kept cattle, sheep and goats and would certainly have been the first pastoralists to venture south of northern Kenya. Two exciting digs, at Gol Kopjes and at a rock shelter in the kopjes around the Serengeti Research Institute at Seronera, have indicated, however, that a hunter-gatherer lifestyle was still practiced in addition to pastoralism. The evidence also points to a trans-humant lifestyle, with wet seasons being devoted almost entirely to pastoralism on the eastern plains around Gol Kopjes and dry seasons spent in the woodlands around Seronera where hunting and gathering was practiced to supplement the diet. This is shown by the higher proportion of wild animal bones to domesticated animal remains at Seronera. These people buried their dead under stone cairns, used decorated pottery, and made use of stone pestles, mortars, and bowls. Stone pendants, mollusc and ostrich shell fragments, and the remains of red ochre suggest that body adornment was also practiced. The Stone Bowl people may also have been the first to regularly burn the grasslands, a practice which led to the fire climax vegetation seen in the Serengeti today.

Many questions about the Pastoral Neolithic era remain unanswered. For example, what were the stone circles on the western side of a number of kopjes that have been attributed to the Pastoral Neolithic era? Were they the foundation for some

Pages 40–41: Bush fire

Pages 42–43: Impala herd

Pages 44–45: Moru Kopjes

human or animal brushwood shelters, or did they have some magic-religious significance? A similar mystery surrounds the famous rock gongs, the best known example being found at Moru. Rows of perfectly symmetric cup-shaped depressions in the rock produce a remarkable variety of musical notes when struck. Are these stunning scoresheets in stone, or more prosaically, are they like the "talking" drums of the Ashanti, carrying messages or warnings? It is pertinent to note that rock gongs are not unique to the Serengeti. They have been found all over Africa, from Nigeria to the Transvaal and on islands in Lake Victoria, as well as in Scotland and France. Dr. Mary Leakey believes the rock gongs may predate the Pastoral Neolithic and suggests they may be associated with the creators of the rock paintings found at Kondoa in central Tanzania. The association of rock gongs with rock paintings has also been documented at Birnin Kudu in Nigeria, and it is conceivable that they may have provided music for a religious cult.

Most of the rock art in the kopje areas of the Serengeti was almost certainly done in the last five hundred years by pastoralists. The only well-known exception is a concentric circle image in white on a rock shelter roof in Moru which may be several thousand years old. It is not known whether this art is of Pastoral Neolithic origin or by preceding Late Stone Age peoples. In terms of technological ability, any of the Late Stone Age peoples could have made rock gongs, and the same can also be said of the bao gaming boards found on many of the kopjes, each consisting of two or four parallel rows of shallow, round holes drilled into a smooth face of flat rock. Stone tools and implements found throughout the Late Stone Age are virtually identical regardless of the culture with which they are associated.

The Iron Age is the first of the metallurgical periods in East Africa's prehistory and even then is very late on the scene. In the Serengeti it begins around 1300 years ago, coinciding with the disappearance of the Stone Bowl people. Apart from a few arrowheads, very few iron artifacts have been found, but numerous whetstones worn into the rock of many kopjes attest to the sharpening of iron implements during this period. Although the identity of these early Iron Age people in the Serengeti is not known for certain, it is thought they were probably bands of Nilotic people moving in from the north,

perhaps dispersing from the Sudanic Nile region as a result of competition over diminishing resources. The Nilotic Maa-speaking peoples are the final inheritors of this tradition, having entered the Serengeti within the last five hundred years, but their precursors may have been early Tatog people now living south of the Serengeti around Mount Hanang. Traditionally feared by the Masai who, otherwise, were the scourge of the East African highlands until the late nineteenth century, the Tatog were known in the past to perform fertility ceremonies in the Ngorongoro Crater at a striking grove of fig trees that almost certainly were planted there for this very purpose. The giant, lonely fig tree east of the Barafu Kopjes in the Serengeti may also have originated in this way, both instances perhaps providing evidence of a Tatog presence in these areas before the coming of the Masai.

Finally, despite the coming of the pastoralists, it should not be thought that the hunter-gatherer bands were forced out of the Serengeti. Small groups of Ndorobo hunter-gatherers lived throughout the area until 1953 (and the Masai until 1959). These bands would have traded with incoming pastoralists much as the Ndorobo, more recently, have provided the Masai with pottery, ironware, and honey.

Footprints in the petrified ash at Laetoli, a lava stone circle on the shores of Lake Olduvai, the chords of a forgotten cult hammered in a spall of granite at Moru Kopjes, all are lithic reminders of the past that are keys to the present. To sit on Gong Rock at Moru looking out across the plains towards Naabi Hill is to be reminded that the vista is virtually unchanged over the past four million years. This is largely due to the dominating influence of the volcanoes and a climate that has changed little and, when it has, has done so gradually. Consequently, the great web of life on the savannah, the whole intricate network of interrelationships between soil and vegetation, vegetation and herbivore, herbivore and carnivore, has co-evolved over an immense span of time. What we are privileged to observe and experience, therefore, is a completely natural ecosystem. Ice caps have never frozen this ancient landscape, nor has the sea ever reclaimed it, nor has forest covered it since *Australopithecus* left his footprints in the ashes of Laetoli. The Serengeti is a window into time, taking us back to our beginnings.

ALLAN EARNSHAW

Page 47: Olduvai Gorge

Pages 48–49: One of the last great elephant herds in the Serengeti

Page 50: Wildebeest and Lemagrut Mountain

Page 51: Zebras on the slopes of Lemagrut Mountain

Pages 52–53: Thunderstorm

Pages 54–55: Cheetah on a kopje at Gol

CYCLED RHYTHMS

The road from Arusha skirts the southern rim of the crater, dips down to cross the Olduvai Gorge, then up again. A mile or two further on it tops a rise and, suddenly, before it lies a sea.

This sea can be the brightest green, dun-colored, or golden brown, at other times, strangely pink, or even blackened by fire, all according to season. The eye sweeps from the north round to the southwest, taking in this sea—of grass.

Nine out of ten overland travelers come upon the Serengeti by this route, and it provides the most riveting of introductions. Around 6,000 feet at the top of the rise, the whole panorama tilts gently westward as far as the eye can see and, beyond, dropping to about 4,000 feet where the plain marches with the unseen shores of Lake Victoria, 150 miles away.

As I came this way, the first bird to catch my eye on the Serengeti Plain was an ostrich. The sight seemed apt. It came as no great surprise that out of a total of some 460 bird species to be found in this part of Tanzania, the first that actually presented itself should be the world's largest. Legs pounding like pistons, it paced beside the Land Rover, doughnuts of dust bursting from the heels at every stride, for this was the dry season.

Ostrich statistics always pop up on these occasions. The tallest bird of course, at eight feet, and the biggest too, at 300 pounds, it is the fastest running bird at a possible forty knots, if sufficiently pressed. Less well known is the size of the ostrich's eye, said to be the largest eye of any land animal and larger by far than its brain! Indeed, the endearingly detached expression sometimes suggests this could be so.

But once upon a time, ostriches flew. Back in the evolution of reptiles into birds, a fowl developed—the ancestor of the ostrich. It was a sizable bird without doubt, and certainly a bird of the plains. Its flight may have posed few threats to an albatross, but on a Wilbur Wright sort of level, and when inclination stirred within its ample breast, it could

Pages 56–57: Wildebeest crossing the Mara River

Pages 58–59: Galloping wildebeest

Pages 60–61: Leopard with cub

become airborne, and remain so, for an appreciable period.

As millennia passed, stalking the level ground, foraging widely and with ease for food that was plentiful, the creature lost the need and even the desire for flight. Legs developed both length and strength and the wings atrophied, to finally produce the familiar and much-loved ratite of today. Yesterday's wings are today's extravagant steadying sails, cooling fans, or shade-casting parasols for the young. The ostrich's way of life has more in common with antelope than anything in the feathered world.

By now my ostrich had set course to the south, distorted by shimmering heat and distance but keeping the same unpressured stride. Dignity and freedom on the hoof. A bird shaped by the plains themselves.

Despite its resemblance to a sea, it is convenient to think of the Serengeti in another sense—as an island. Today it stands out as an island of zoological plenty, surrounded by areas of similar topographical aspect, but areas now fallen victim to the encroachment of man and all his works. Sadly, the island is a small one, but large enough nevertheless to goad the imagination to picture the days when the entire central belt of Africa stretching from the east coast to the west, from the Congo in the north to the Zambezi, offered the same spectacle of massed wild animals about their business. It is an area some 1600 miles east to west and 1000 miles north to south—savannah country. In Tanzania, it is called *Miombo.*

It is unlikely that in those earlier times, the herds on the Serengeti we know were any larger—there were just more "Serengetis," spread like lily pads on a pond, across the scene. Some would have touched, natural barriers would have distanced others. The arcane cycles of animal movement, dictated by grazing, will have followed much the same pattern—each species taking what was best for its needs from a given place, then moving on. The grass yield of the Serengeti will have varied over the years, then as now, but there was probably never enough to have supported materially larger numbers of game.

So a species found its own population level in accordance with the bounty of the land. Natural checks exerted themselves. Predators took their prescribed toll. The rains would sometimes fail. Though fluctuations would be inevitable, today's count of ungulates in the Serengeti area could well be within a few percent of the population strength of a century and a half ago.

"Migration" and "Serengeti" are all but synonymous. If one accepts that the latter still provides the arena for the world's greatest concentration of large and constantly moving wild animals, it follows that it will find honorable mention in every dissertation on the former. Moreover, the Serengeti must be loosely taken to include the Masai Mara Game Reserve, across the border in Kenya, as well as the Loita Plains and the Crater Highlands, featuring Ngorongoro. Everything that affects migration here begins with rain. And everything that involves weather, in any of its manifestations, carries built-in uncertainties of timing, place, and duration.

The dry season can be said to extend from July to November, the "long rains," December to May. So the plains which first feel the effects of the dry-up see the exodus of their ungulate animals in May or June. Zebra and wildebeest are in the lead, the rest follow, leaving a brown and deserted landscape to the dust-devils that cavort in the far distance. But there is always movement somewhere, a group of Grant's gazelle reluctant to follow the herds, a solitary jackal fossicking about, its very loneliness catching the eye. There is always something; magic remains the year round.

By now, many of the great herds will be down to the west, scattered over the lower Mara River system and the more fertile areas that border Speke Gulf of Lake Victoria. These are tsetse fly lands, ironically protecting the wild plains game against human settlement and massed encroachment of domestic livestock.

The first rains to break the drought are often the heaviest and may build in the offing as early as October. They appear in the north—gigantic piles of cloud—heaving themselves out of the hot and shimmering air. They grow before the eyes like splendid white cauliflowers from a dark and menacing base and spend their energy in downpour. At night they flicker from within, their outlines sharply delineated by incessant lighting, as they slowly move south, drenching the desiccated earth.

Then comes the life-giving smell of slaked soil. Immediately thereafter, plants begin to appear—the brightest of new grass, dotted with little white Ramphicarpa flowers.

March and April can see heavy downpours, too.

Page 63: Phalanx of migrating wildebeest and zebras

Pages 64–65: Masai ostriches, Ngorongoro Crater

The average annual rainfall amounts to about thirty inches and sometimes a third of this total will fall in these two months alone. As the grass follows the rain, the animals follow the grass and, once more, the plain's game is in motion, returning to the areas that not many months ago saw them leave.

Zebras consume the longest and coarsest growth. Wildebeest, hartebeest, and gazelle follow, the preferred grass texture for each animal established by the earlier cropping. Because there is still land in plenty and a system in balance, they move on without overgrazing, allowing the grass to regenerate.

When drought sets in again, the southeast of the Serengeti is the first to feel its impact, and once more the exodus begins. From the air, one can see the ritual resuming as black lines of wildebeest start to form. From such a vantage point, they look like safari ants in their tens of thousands, bunching tightly to pass through some constriction, fanning out again over the wide ground, leaving tracks that are easily visible long after the beasts have passed.

These migrations resemble a ritual walkabout—circuitous, a little unpredictable, and apparently aimless. Minor local movements occur within the larger picture. A short dry spell in the middle of the rains, when animals are grazing the sweetest grass on the shallowest top-soils, will trigger a local movement out of harmony with the general trend. Such occurences can be expected between the Maswa Reserve to the southwest and the Ngorongoro Conservation Area to the southeast of the Serengeti National Park. It is here that wildebeest will calve in January and February when grazing is at its best.

Though it may appear aimless to a casual observer, to witness the wildebeest migration—especially if near a swollen river—leaves no doubt about the true extent of the animal's zeal. The frenzied fervor, a rampage of creatures possessed, is somehow rendered more poignant by the lugubrious expressions of the wildebeest themselves.

They are totally committed to reaching point B from point A, oblivious to the risk of drowning on a holocaust scale. A collective imperative has charge of them, any individuality is immersed in the hysteria of the mass. Sustained pressure from the rear overwhelms the animals in front and they must go for it—to the furthest bank and then press on. Somewhere beyond is where they need to be. The grass is greener . . .

Opportunist crocodiles claim a number of beasts, the brimming river takes many as well, but most of the wildebeest make it. They file on, more relaxed now, while at the crossing and further downstream the drowned victims wash onto sandbars or hook on overhanging branches, and the carrion feast begins.

Soon the carcasses will be bloated with putrefaction, a-buzz with flies and no longer attracting vultures, too gorged to retain interest. The birds wheel around overhead or sit, hunch-shouldered, in surrounding trees, loath to leave the wake but wanting no more of it. A jackal passes, looks, and passes on, replete as the birds.

This exodus is surely the most stupendous of all dramas in the animal kingdom, enacted with a cast of a million. Yet as the tragedy plays itself out on its horrendous scale, there is another, gentler, side to the Serengeti. A furtive dik-dik, in some shady corner, marks and watches over his territory. Content to stay within its boundaries, he feels no urge whatsoever to leave his own little chosen acre of Africa.

With so much available meat, about twenty-five species for the taking, the big mammalian predators live an easy life. Local lions are famed as much for their indolence as their looks, enjoying the laid-back lifestyle only ease and plenty can provide. A Serengeti lion, according to records, averages over twenty hours out of twenty-four either resting or actually sleeping. The remaining hours are concerned, to a varying degree, with food—its acquisition and consumption.

A single lion is said to eat—allowing for proverbially irregular meals—an average of ten pounds of meat a day. The total take of meat in a year by all the major predators, lions, leopards, cheetahs, hyenas, and hunting-dogs, amounts to 20,000,000 pounds! Yet this seemingly astronomic harvest represents less than one-tenth of the ungulate biomass on the plains. Furthermore, in accord with the whole paradoxical nature of animal predation—survival of the fittest—the hunter bestows upon the hunted the reward of improving its stock and enhancing the survival values of its species to the enduring benefit of both parties.

In open country like this, such finely tuned interaction is easy to watch and more readily understood. The food chains, the pecking orders, are daily happenings for all to see—from the king of beasts to the little denizens of the grass roots. At this end of the scale, one may turn over a dried animal dropping to find a dung beetle at work, enjoying the bounty of an end product before unseen subtleties of organic chemistry take over to nourish the surrounding vegetation.

There is no leaving the Serengeti without mentioning the kopjes—the "inselbergs" or "island mountains." These striking features rise from the plains in upward thrusting jumbles of granite rock, interrupting the broad and sweeping lines of the landscape with sharply angular accents. Little ecosystems all their own, they support vegetation as well as animals. Kopjes offer cameos of specialized African life in a unique habitat, against a mosaic of leaves and among fortresses of rock, in sunshine and the deepest shade.

A rock hyrax, with whiskers a-twitch, peeps from a crevice a foot or two away. A gaudy agama lizard scuttles over the warming boulders and pauses for morning press-ups.

The extraordinary pancake tortoises live here, flat and flexible as their name implies and no doubt just as palatable to a predator. When danger threatens, rather than retract the head and feet as others of their kind, they make with full speed for the nearest rock crevice where the evolutionary secret of their shape is immediately revealed. Here they will slide like a posted letter into the sanctuary of a crack too narrow for serious pursuit.

Diligent search could find a fifteen-foot rock python, beautifully marked and thick as a man's thigh. In the bushes a chameleon could be poised, still as a statue but for the swiveling turret of an eye, green as the leaves, grey or brown as the stems, nature's perfect color simulator.

A fragrant jasmine blooms here; and one of the world's most gorgeous wild flowers, the flame-colored climbing lily, *Gloriosa Superba*. And sometimes a lion or leopard will pose as king-of-the-castle on the topmost rock, presenting against the dawn or sunset the classic silhouette of majesty and dominion.

But what of the future? The "island" of the Serengeti Plain is under direst threat. Because it can only be considered, ecologically, in conjunction with the Masai Mara, two nations are involved. Affluent Kenya and economically depressed Tanzania face each other across a troubled border of which the animals know nothing as they follow their seasonal migrations, but which could so easily bring about their demise. Agricultural pressures, bureaucracy, and local politics beset the north. Governmental apathy and negligence, leading to poaching on an industrial scale, mark the south. To all practical purposes, the black rhinoceros is already doomed, the elephant close on its tail.

The Serengeti-Mara cries out for a unified management, with power and courage, a level horizon, and sufficient sense of urgency to bury national and tribal prejudice and see the place for what it is—a world heritage. It is a cohesive whole that must be administered as such if it is to survive. Neither side of the political border can make it alone.

Over the years a host of zoologists and game wardens have dedicated their energies to this fabled place, to save, watch over, and learn from it, and apply its manifold lessons of conservation worldwide. Serengeti is a treasure-house, unique and irreplaceable.

If you take the same road out again—the ostrich road—which leads towards Arusha, it skirts the crater rim of Ngorongoro where stands a memorial stone to one of the many whose names have become linked with Serengeti in their own special way. He was killed in a flying accident while making a routine census of game on the plains. The work was nearly done and a fair proportion of a young and promising life had been devoted to it.

"MICHAEL GRZIMEK, 12.4.1934–10.1.1959" runs the inscription. "He gave all he possessed for the wild animals of Africa, including his life."

There is much to reflect upon when leaving this place; and not the least of which is that the continued health of the Serengeti is every bit as vital to the human species as well—whatever the cost.

KEITH SHACKLETON

Pages 68–69: Rhinoceros with calf, Ngorongoro Crater

Pages 70–71: Lioness in an acacia tree

Page 72: *Crowned cranes*
Page 73: *Gol Kopjes*
Pages 74–75: *Lions fighting*

Page 76: Big-maned lion

Page 77: Lion face to face with Egyptian cobra

Pages 78–79: Zebras at dusk

Pages 80–81: Fever trees, Ngare Nanyuki River

*Page 82 (above): Cory Bustard
displaying to attract a mate*

Page 82 (below): Serval

82   *Pages 82–83: Leopard and cub*

Page 84: Python in a tree

Page 85: Python after killing a Thompson's gazelle

Pages 86–87: Zebras

Page 88 (above): Lions feeding on a zebra
Page 88 (below): Vultures on a zebra kill
Page 89: Crocodile feeding on a drowned zebra
Pages 90–91: Mara River during the rains

Page 92: Cheetah with impala fawn

Page 93: Giraffes in courtship

Page 94: Ancient giant fig tree in the Serengeti

Page 95: Owl poised in a kopje

Page 96 (above): Male impalas
Page 96 (below): Thompson gazelles sparring
Page 97: Grant gazelles

Pages 98–99: Zebras fighting

Page 100: Lion cubs

Page 101: Flowering lily at Gol Kopjes

Page 102: Rock hyraxes, denizens of the kopjes

Pages 102–103: Cheetah

Pages 104–105: Wildebeest skulls on Lake Ndutu's soda encrusted shore

Pages 106–107: Lions in repose
Page 107: Lion and cubs

PRESERVING THE SERENGETI

The Chief Park Warden of the Serengeti showed me his favorite place in the entire park one day. We set off early from headquarters at Seronera, out the road to the Western Corridor, then north to the banks of the Grumeti River. As we got out of the Land Rover, the Warden motioned for quiet and whispered that we should tiptoe as best we could. He led the way, carrying his gun, and soon pointed to the sight that thrilled him most in this domain of 5,600 square miles—three huge, basking crocodiles, the longest at least twelve feet, loafing in reptilian bliss on a narrow sand finger in the shallows. The fun of surprising these locally famous Grumeti crocs was the Warden's idea of the most special gift that he could present to a visitor. Then the Warden chuckled, prompting the crocs to melt off the sandbar into the water in one fluid motion, and he wished aloud that he could make this trip more often. We drove further up the line of the river to a lovely spot for a picnic. It was a relaxed moment, full of camaraderie, but it would precede long hours of serious conversation about the current state of the park's vehicles and equipment, water lines, anti-poaching operations, whatever it took to make the Serengeti, indeed any national park in East Africa, run for another week, another month, another year.

That year was 1981, and the Chief Park Warden was David Stephens Babu, the first African warden of the Serengeti. He held the office for nine years, and I, in my professional capacity, spent time with him over the course of seven of them. David was always animated, often passionate when he talked shop, exceedingly gracious, generous, and brave, even while almost always feeling frustrated.

Since the early 1900s, the human landscape of the Serengeti has been thick with individuals traveling and working there in the name of conservation. The Germans got there first. In 1892, an explorer named Baumann walked from the Indian Ocean coast, up

Pages 108–109: Safari vehicle

Pages 110–111: Zebras at dusk

the lip of Ngorongoro Crater and then down to camp on the crater floor. Having shot three rhinos in one day, he intimates that he could have shot more had he been a keener hunter. He recorded the first sightings of Lakes Eyasi, Manyara, and Ndutu, the latter lying slightly to the south of the Serengeti's Central Plains. His party took twenty-three days to march through Serengeti to Lake Victoria.

Next to record his trek through the area was another German, a geographer named Jaeger. He wrote in his journal in 1907, "grass, grass, grass, grass and grass. One looks around and sees only grass and sky." Rinderpest and reputedly hostile tribes had long deterred travelers from penetrating further into the center of an area considered "unfit for human habitation." These first intrepid Europeans lifted the curtain on the Serengeti ecosystem.

The hunters followed, and keen is hardly the word to describe their zeal. Their activities reached a zenith in the 1920s as they made the Serengeti world-famous for the big game they came to shoot. Leopards were an easy shot, perched smugly in the yellow fever trees which grow along the Seronera River; but lion hunting was the big draw. Both were considered, in those early days, vermin to be shot on sight. The hunter Saxton Pope wrote about his Serengeti exploits, "We've now shot fifty-two male lions. I think possibly we're overdoing it a bit. Others will be coming after us." Another hunter, mentioned by conservationist Bernhard Grzimek, purportedly shot a hundred lions on his safari, and carried only their tails and a few skins home.

Amateur hunting was unrestricted, and the spoils seemed excessive to some of the early professional hunters. Their complaints prompted the colonial government to set aside nine hundred square miles of the Serengeti as a lion sanctuary in 1929. It was the first glimmer of a conservation policy for the region.

Concurrently, the Serengeti's reputation was being magnified by filmmakers, notably Martin Johnson, who spent three months there in 1928 making a lion film, *Simba*. Lions can still be seen today in those same places depicted in the film. Myles Turner, a hunter and game warden, wrote, "It is said in those days that one merely drove along the Seronera and the lions, hearing the cars, would follow hoping for a meal. Sensational tricks were filmed such as feeding lions in the back of trucks and filming through the rear window of the cab. One film company actually stuffed a human dummy with zebra meat and filmed a lion pulling the body from a tent."[1] In the early 1930s, with hunting along the borders of the sanctuary, occasional filmmaking, and budding tourism all in varying stages of momentum, the Serengeti underwent a transition. New areas, including Ngorongoro Crater, were given protected status, and all legal hunting stopped in 1937 when the Serengeti was made a permanent game reserve.

In 1940 the British made the Serengeti, including the Ngorongoro Crater Highlands, a national park, the first in East Africa. Making a drastic exception to the rule of a true national park, however, they allowed people to remain. Cultivators grew maize and tobacco in the crater, and in the Serengeti proper, the Masai and others with livestock used the area around the Moru Kopjes. Very little administrative action was taken for the next ten years as the fragile soils and vegetation were dug, trampled, and chopped.

In 1951 authority for managing the park was vested in a board of trustees whose concerns for preserving its wildlife potential began to prevail. Revised and extended boundaries were declared, but they would remain tenuous for years to come. In the Moru Kopjes there were a hundred families of Ndorobo with 18,000 head of livestock. Through combined pressure from park authorities, Masai elders, and the Tanzanian government, they were forced out of the area in 1953. Several years later the Masai, themselves, would feel the brunt of similar pressure.

The park's integrity was most threatened in 1956 when the Tanganyika Legislative Council produced a White Paper on the Serengeti National Park. It stated that the presence of Masai in the park was not considered an intrusion and made the promise that their rights would not be disturbed without their consent. The trustees were horrified. They insisted the pastoralists be persuaded to leave the park, but the Masai would only agree to boundaries that fell far short of what the authorities wanted. The impasse created frustration and bitter feelings on both sides.

The government proposed an alternate solution which involved setting aside three areas within the existing park to be free of all human interference: Ngorongoro Crater, Empakai Crater, and the Western Serengeti. To compensate, they proposed excising the area called the Central Plains and returning it to the Masai. This included the magnificent Moru Kopjes, the very heart of the wildebeest calving area, and implied that people and livestock would be there in perpetuity, a prospect the conservationists deplored.

By now the Serengeti had captured the world's imagination, and outcries from England, the United States, and the rest of East Africa stirred the government to postpone any action pending further investigation. In late 1956, a Professor Pearsall was engaged by the Fauna and Flora Preservation Society of England to carry out an ecological survey of the Serengeti and to produce a report with recommendations which would resolve the boundary controversy. He stressed three criteria for settling the problem: the protected area be sufficient to include the entire cycle of migratory movement; the wildlife and the Masai occupy separate territories; and attention be paid to the broad ecological potential within the region such as water catchment areas, fragile soils, and shade-giving woodlands. The acceptance of Pearsall's report meant another reprieve, albeit brief, for the Serengeti. A final round of controversy would be played out within a year.

In 1957 the Governmental Committee of Enquiry was appointed to decide upon the fate of the Serengeti. After touring the whole area, they supported retaining the Central Plains, extending the park northward, and eliminating human settlement within those boundaries. The committee decided to set aside Olduvai Gorge and the Ngorongoro Crater Highlands as a conservation area which would support the multiple uses of tourism, conservation, and pastoralism. The Serengeti's Central Plains had emerged intact, and this was most important.

Myles Turner went to Tanganyika in 1956 to be Warden in charge of the Western Serengeti. It would be his third career, preceded by one as game control officer in Kenya and another as a professional hunter. Now he would spend years working to preserve the very animals he had formerly hunted.

In the early part of his stay in the Serengeti, Turner devoted himself to an all-out effort to contain the rampant poaching. He recruited and trained a field force of game rangers to defend the Serengeti's boundaries, and led those men for the next sixteen years. Life consisted of erecting guard posts, mounting ambushes, carrying out dawn raids on villages around the park periphery, flying aerial reconnaisances, and countless patrols. The hazards encountered, however, were not only human—patrols on foot often brought one face to face with rhino or buffalo. The grit and tenacity required to do this sort of work year in and year out made Turner one of the legendary wardens in Africa's conservation history. That he was a consummate diarist with a sense of history merits the gratitude of anyone interested in learning about the Serengeti.

When Turner and his wife came to the Serengeti, Colonel P. G. Malloy was Director of National Parks. Based on the outcome of an anti-poaching sweep carried out by Turner and his colleague, Gordon Poolman, during which they collected over one thousand wire snares, Colonel Molloy extrapolated that 150,000 animals were being slaughtered annually by poaching gangs. The poachers' main methods of killing consisted of laying steel wire snares which could cause brutally prolonged suffering before death; or poisoned arrows, so lethal that a man whose flesh was grazed by one stood little chance of living for another forty minutes. Despite their grisly methods, some of the poachers had to be grudgingly respected for their bushcraft and for the fearlessness with which they made their living. Turner's admiration for certain individuals, often reciprocated, was forged through repeated encounters over many years.

The time from 1960 to the mid-1970s was the most exciting in Serengeti's conservation history. Those were the years of building a park, of fighting the poachers, of beginning to unravel the dynamics of the great migration, and of raising money to support the whole enterprise. Conservation giants, both expatriate and Tanzanian, participated.

John Owen was Director of National Parks at the time the colonial administration was relinquishing its control to the independent government of Tanzania. Described as avuncular, soft-spoken, and highly energetic, he was an orchestrator possessed with a vision for the Serengeti, and his audiences seemed to share it, for they gave generously. Owen performed a tour de force in the garnering of resources, unprecedented and rarely surpassed since then. He raised the money and amassed the equipment—planes, cars, trucks, graders, building materials—to transform rough dirt tracks into passable

roads, enabling his wardens to cover ground further and faster than before as they and their ranger teams battled against the endless tide of poachers.

Another giant of the era was Bernhard Grzimek. Professor Grzimek's dreams for the Serengeti merged with John Owen's, and he was able to fuel their mutual vision with prodigious contributions of cash. A powerful fund raiser and totally dedicated to speaking on behalf of animals, Grzimek's stature was confirmed by African politicians who always welcomed him into their offices.

Professor Grzimek had recreated the Frankfurt Zoo from the rubble of the Second World War. His son Michael's travels in Africa fired the father's sense of mission. Both father and son felt that if the Serengeti were to remain intact, it should be scrutinized and understood. They learned to fly and, in December 1957, Grzimek, 48, and his son set off across Europe and down the length of Africa bound for the Serengeti, in a Dornier aircraft stylishly painted with zebra stripes. The Grzimeks pioneered aerial survey techniques, learning along the way to perfect their estimates of animal numbers by using transects. They sent thousands of plant and soil samples to Europe for analysis and observed animals' migratory habits. The father and son team spent a year working in the Serengeti. On the day before they were to depart, Michael was killed when a vulture collided with the wing of their striped aircraft. Their reputation had relied on work carried out thoroughly and painstakingly, a seminal contribution to the research potential that would, in 1958, inspire the creation of the Michael Grzimek Memorial Laboratory.

A book and film, both titled *Serengeti Shall Not Die*, catapulted the elder Grzimek into the public eye. For a man of his conviction, ego, and sheer physical presence, that was the right place to be. He became a media personality with a regular zoo and wildlife television program. His instinct for working an audience resulted in the collection of millions of deutsche marks for the cause of wildlife, the bulk of it for his beloved Serengeti.

Twenty years ago, when the concept of grass roots conservation programs for the benefit of Africa was embryonic, Grzimek did not wait to see if the bandwagon was going to roll. He gave, and gave big. Conversations with the man were markedly one-sided (his), but he noticed, or osmosed, signs of an idea whose time had come. He poured thousands

into the burgeoning Wildlife Clubs movement in Kenya. Two decades later that prototype stands as one of many testimonials to his support and faith in modern Africa.

By 1962, Myles Turner's anti-poaching units had become much more sophisticated in their activities. The use of aircraft and ground vehicles afforded them increased mobility, and management possessed a much better understanding of migration patterns. But there could be no letup in their operations. Turner's annual report figures through the 1960s showed clearly that poaching had not leveled off and that more captures were occurring inside the park. His statistics implied that pressure on the park would increase as game was exterminated outside its boundaries. "Unless there was a radical change of attitude towards conservation among the people bordering the Serengeti, the animals would never be safe. So long as they regarded it as a right to kill animals in the park, and viewed national park staff as enemies of the public, force alone would never be able to protect the wildlife of the Serengeti."

The Serengeti ranks as one of the most studied ecosystems on the planet. The Grzimek father and son team had set an example for droves of investigators when they carried out their painstaking surveys in 1958. The continuing need to understand the workings of the Serengeti created the momentum to transform the Michael Grzimek Memorial Laboratory into the Serengeti Research Institute in 1966.

The late 1960s and early 1970s were the halcyon years for wildlife research in East Africa. Later on, when so much "crisis conservation" prevailed, research would be discouraged, in a backlash of misguided sentiment which held that there was no more time for study, only time to fight a rearguard action to save wildlife in East Africa. In 1966, however, all was well. Tanzania National Parks, with John Owen directing, created the Serengeti Research Institute (SRI) as a base where teams of scientists could unravel the complexities and tune into the cyclic, biological rhythms of this unique ecosystem.

Under the leadership of its first scientific director, Dr. Hugh Lamprey, the institute hummed with the comings and goings of a large group of scientists from the United States and Europe. They were lured by the uniqueness of a relatively unaltered ecosystem—large enough to allow flexibility for conserving what was within it—and seduced by its beauty.

Their purpose was to monitor the park and advise the authorities on management. A research center was constructed positioned around the bases of the kopjes in the interest of maintaining a low human profile.

As the years rolled by, the original core of scientists illuminated our knowledge of how the Serengeti ecosystem works. Some of them went on to become very powerful forces for conservation today. For example, Dr. George Schaller carried out his exemplary studies of lions and their prey between 1966 and 1969, learning more about lion behavior than had ever been known before. By his example—that of studying one area or species for years at a time—he fostered a new approach to conservation, one that is now termed "conservation biology." Says Schaller, "You can say it in three words: conservation through science. The biologists go into the field and collect scientifically precise information about the ecosystem in which they work. . . . We take this knowledge and we try to find some way to use it for the common good of the country in which we work . . . to direct conservation of resources, to help human need, to help local people sustain the environment."[2]

Throughout the early 1970s, visiting scientists from all over the world probed the Serengeti. Dr. Harvey Croze observed the impact of elephants on woodlands; Dr. Michael Norton-Griffiths studied the implications of shifts in animal populations, especially wildebeests. Individual species were studied: hyenas and hyraxes, giraffes and gazelles, dik-diks and termites. SRI research projects were financed by considerable backing from a half dozen international conservation agencies in the United States, Canada, and Germany. The largesse attracted by the scientists' activities spilled over to benefit the park with such items as vehicles for anti-poaching operations. Funds provided in 1962 by the New York Zoological Society allowed the park to purchase a wedge of land along the Kenya border, the Lamai, which was critical to the wildebeest migration.

Wildlife research in the Serengeti wound down in the mid-1970s. Tanzania, by then, was in the process of Africanization, a movement to replace expatriates with nationals. This resulted in the premature withdrawal of formidable research expertise and funding for SRI. In 1977, when Tanzania closed its border with Kenya in response to political differences, the conservation infrastructure of Tanzania was further isolated, particularly from the practical resources emanating from Kenya. Reduced to a skeleton staff, SRI resembled a ghost town. A few people continued their research, and the African Wildlife Foundation provided fuel and vehicle spare parts to enable rangers to read far flung rain gauges month in and month out, thus enabling two decades worth of data collection to continue. Dr. A. R. E. Sinclair, with support from the New York Zoological Society, has continued annual monitoring of wildebeests since 1966 in the longest ongoing study ever conducted on a large ungulate population. In 1980, SRI's concept and infrastructure were altered to encompass research stations in several parks and reserves.

In 1972, swept along in the tide of Africanization, Myles Turner handed over charge of the Serengeti field force to a citizen warden. Before his death in 1984, Turner provided us with an insightful footnote to his Serengeti experience. "After reading this account of more than a decade of anti-poaching in the Serengeti, the reader may well wonder how it is that any game has survived the years of unremitting carnage. There are three main reasons. Firstly, sheer numbers alone have, until now, defied every effort at extermination. Secondly, every year for up to six months at a time, the great wildebeest and zebra herds are scattered far and wide across the central and eastern plains, many miles from the nearest village and therefore relatively safe from poaching. Thirdly, the presence of the tsetse fly—which has been called the 'greatest conservationist in Africa'—has resisted any attempts at settlement and cultivation. But as Tanzania's rapidly increasing human population closes in on all sides, denying wild land formerly accessible to the wanderings of migratory herds, pressure will continue to grow in the years to come."[3]

True to Turner's prediction, human population pressure on parks has escalated rapidly in East Africa and nowhere more so than in Kenya which shares the ecosystem that comprises the Serengeti-Mara. Though only 540 square miles in area, compared to the Serengeti's 5,600 square miles, the Masai Mara Game Reserve is crucial to the annual wildebeest migration for a third of each year. The migration must move over a large enough area to allow for habitat recovery and, without the safety valve of the Mara's grasslands, Serengeti's landscape would be denuded by overgrazing.

The Masai Mara is what many would conjure up

if asked to describe their vision of a wildlife paradise. Studded with patches of woodland, its rolling grasslands are beautiful and inviting as are the chic, comfortable tourist lodges and tented camps dotted about the reserve. Add a luxuriant, cool, riverine forest snaking through the prime scenic area which, for several months of the year, holds the largest concentration of predators and plains game on earth, and you have the place that visitors want to return to year after year.

For a very long time, the Mara was avoided by man and wildlife alike. It was a haven for the tsetse fly which causes sleeping sickness in people and animals, particularly domestic stock. In the 1950s, the Serengeti herds did not migrate as far north as the Mara because their smaller population (250,000 animals at that time) had plenty of grass at hand. That situation changed for several reasons. When domestic stock were inoculated against rinderpest in the 1950s, the disease receded among wild animal populations as well, and their numbers rose. Wildlife, and Masai with their burgeoning cattle herds, made incursions onto lands they had formerly avoided because of the tsetse fly. Constant trampling by animal hooves prevented young tree seedlings from reaching maturity, which resulted in the gradual disappearance of woodlands and thick bush—tsetse habitat—and the increase of nourishing grasslands. In time, the ecosystem had changed radically. The Mara had become prime grazing land.

The Mara was set aside as a wildlife sanctuary in 1948 and upgraded to a national reserve in 1961. Unlike most national parks and reserves, however, ownership of the land is retained by the Masai whose interests are defended by a local county council. The profits from gate receipts and royalties generated through tourism in the Mara are intended to benefit the Masai through community development such as schools and health facilities. This system is vulnerable to corruption and mismanagement, and many Masai feel they do not benefit enough from the profits. Without compelling incentives, the Masai have little reason to tolerate competition with hundreds of thousands of wild animals for land and water. Only with astute management and practical results can this profit-circulating system bear fruit for all concerned.

There are other pressures which are equally daunting. Tourism, the goose that lays the golden egg, sometimes seems on the verge of destroying the source of its revenue—the land and its inhabitants. The habitat is being degraded by heavy traffic and off-road driving, and the animals are often disturbed by the throngs of eager visitors. This has become such a problem in the Mara that outside agencies have been called in to evaluate the damage and make recommendations.

Agricultural schemes, crucial to Kenya's self-sufficiency in feeding its burgeoning population, has dealt a further blow to the sanctity of the Mara. Large-scale wheat farms at the northern periphery of the reserve provide a quarter of the country's grain and threaten to cross the Mara's boundaries. Cattle ranching is another threat. As Masai take title deeds to huge expanses of formerly communal ranchland, their demands become more strident for contained wildlife and wildlife-free ranches. With proper incentives—grazing compensation, photographic fees, or water piped to marginal areas—the Masai landowners could tolerate coexistence with wildlife as they did for centuries past.

All these conflicting demands—agriculture, population growth, ranching, tourism, wildlife conservation—culminate in an unenviable dilemma for the governments of wildlife-rich countries. They must be praised for the relatively huge tracts under protected status and the implied commitment to maintaining these magnificent places for themselves and the world. Tanzania has set aside fully twelve percent of its lands as parks and wildlife or forest reserves; Kenya, an admirable nearly five and one-half percent.[4] Praise is not enough, however. As a world heritage, the Serengeti-Mara's survival depends on the world's commitment to helping those countries sustain it. In the short term, money for equipment and anti-poaching can stem the destruction. For the long term, only the satisfaction of basic needs and education can lift people to a level that frees them for the task of conservation.

SANDY PRICE

1. Myles Turner, *My Serengeti Years* (New York: Hamish Hamilton, 1987), p. 37.
2. George B. Schaller quote from the drafted script for a New York Zoological Society Film about Wildlife Conservation International.
3. Myles Turner, op. cit., p. 197.
4. Figures drawn from IUCN report, 1987.

MICHAEL GRZIMEK
12. 4. 1934 — 10. 1. 1959
HE GAVE ALL HE POSSESSED
INCLUDING HIS LIFE
FOR THE WILD ANIMALS OF AFRICA

PROFESSOR BERNHARD GRZIMEK
1909 – 1987

A LIFETIME OF CARING
FOR WILD ANIMALS
AND THEIR PLACE ON OUR PLANET
"IT IS BETTER TO LIGHT A CANDLE
THAN TO CURSE THE DARKNESS"

Page 121: Monument to Michael Grzimek
on the rim of Ngorongoro Crater

Page 122: Wildebeest fording the Mara River

Page 123: Cape buffalo with cattle egrets

Page 124: Waterbuck male

Page 125 (above): Lioness nursing cubs

Page 125 (below): Wildebeest with newborn calf

Pages 126–127: Topis on the plains at sunset

Pages 128–129: Wildebeest crossing Lake Ndutu

Page 130: Gray heron with catfish

Page 131: Hyena

Page 132 (above): Agama lizard atop a buffalo skull
Page 132 (below): Sacred ibis
Page 133: European storks roosting

Page 134: Aloe in flower

Page 135: Lilac-breasted roller

Pages 136–137: Young
lions on the plains

Pages 138–139: Elephants
in Ngorongoro Crater   137

Page 140 (above): Cape buffalo

Page 140 (below): Baboon in the kopjes

Page 141 (above): Wild dogs attacking a wildebeest

Page 141 (below): Black-backed jackal with prey

Page 142: Baboons scaling Nasera Rock

Page 143: Fig tree sending down roots on Nasera Rock

Pages 144–145: Cape chestnut tree with Ngorongoro
Crater in background

SIRENKET

Oh! Ndorror," the old man sighs. He eyes
the pitiable collection of angled bones and
curved horns filing wearily into the thorn
enclosure of Nasera village. The emaciated cattle,
the dry plains whipped with dust by a tireless wind,
and the fetid pools of stagnant river water paint a
familiar picture of Serengeti in the dry season.

Njilalo adjusts his blanket around his shoulders
and resumes his monologue. He blames the wildebeest migration for the cattle's hunger and their lack
of milk. The nutritious grasses, rooted in Pleistocene
volcanic ashes belched up by Tanzania's craters,
Ngorongoro, Lengai, and Empakai, are grazed to a
nub, and the fragile plains are veined with the deep
tracery of hooves. "Say one," he tells me and wags
his finger, a Maasai's[1] way of indicating his first
point has been made. "One," I reply. Worse, he la-
ments, the wildebeest calving has brought fever
which sickens cattle and a taboo has been placed
on the sharing of milk. "Say two," he instructs, scis-
soring two fingers, and I answer, "Two." His voice,
low and measured, drones on and is punctuated by
the refrain *neago ta lelo* ("those are my words").

"But we are not strangers to desperation," Njilalo
says, launching into an *enkiterunoto*, a story of beginnings, a Maasai Genesis tale. "Long ago, hounded
by drought and death, the Maasai left their lands
way to the north and migrated south in search of
pastures. The skies withheld their rains, the old ones
littered the parched route, the women stopped giving birth. It would take a miracle to make the land
green again, to brighten the children's eyes, to bring
milk to the women's breasts. A miracle occurred.
Orkitongoi, the orphan child with a tail, appeared
amidst these wandering wretched, carrying a gourd
of stones and a herding stick. Wherever he struck
his stick, water flowed; where he threw his stones,
white flowers grew. The land soon blossomed with
new grass and flowers, and the cattle were happy."

Page 146: Maasai women

*Pages 148–149: Women carrying sapling
for a circumcision ceremony*

147

Cattle and life, *enkishu*, prospered, Orkitongoi became the first ritual leader, or *Laibon*, and Ndorror endures as the mythic heart and soul of Maasailand.

The Maasai cradle, from whence this migration came, is believed to lie on the southern fringes of the Ethiopian highlands, near the shores of Lake Turkana. We know from archaeological evidence that there were cattle-keeping peoples in the East African interior as far back as 1000 B.C., but pastoralist groups sharing the Maa language only began their trek south in the late 1500s, driving their herds before them. Firmly settled in East Africa's Great Rift Valley by the early seventeenth century, they extended their pasturelands over the next two hundred years, organized in loose territorial alliances, expanding, regrouping, assimilating, and being assimilated.[2]

The beginning of the nineteenth century saw the rise and rapid expansion of one of these groups, the Maasai. In a series of raids they refer to as the "Great Wars," the Maasai consolidated their power over the surrounding peoples by controlling essential resources, particularly dry-season graze and permanent water points. By the 1850s, they occupied 80,000 square miles of East Africa, from Kenya's Lake Baringo south to the Maasai steppe of Tanzania, and soon their hegemony was complete. Credit for their superb organization and stunning victories is given to the great Laibon, Mbatian, a man of legendary stature even today and about whom the elders never tire of talking. "*Eeta oloip*," ("He had shade") Njilalo says, meaning, like a generously branched tree, he attracted great numbers of people.

These victories crowned the golden age of Maasai culture. And then it all changed. Remembering his father's tales, Njilalo pauses, searching deeply in the changing pattern of the fire's embers as if it might finally explain the dramatic shift in fortune. He tells the story of the *olmaitai*, a ten-year cycle of misery and fortune, foretold by the eruption of the volcano Oldoinyo Lengai. It is a Maasai version of Job's story, the introduction to a paradise lost. Pleuropneumonia, followed by a rinderpest pandemic in 1889–1890, draught and locust in 1891, and smallpox in 1892 decimated the Maasai herds by ninety percent and the population by half.[3] "There were women wasted to skeletons from whom the madness of starvation glared . . . 'warriors' scarcely able to crawl

on all fours . . . Parents offered us children to buy for a scrap of meat . . ."[4] Those who survived took refuge with peripheral groups of cultivators and hunters. A succession struggle between Mbatian's sons, Lenana and Senteu, divided the family and led to internal wars. When the Europeans arrived at the turn of the century, the Maasai were in disarray, a shadow of their former selves.

The Maasai-European relationship was rooted from the beginning in mutual admiration and fear. "We say," Njilalo relates, "the warrior, the lion, and the white man are alike." To be respected and even feared, but not trusted. He adds, "They share two other things in common: they both have a mane of hair and, at times, they go crazy in the head."

Betrayed trust became an issue early on between the Maasai and colonial authorities. A treaty drawn up in 1904, creating two reserves in perpetuity for the Kenya Maasai, was breached in 1911 when the British sent the Maasai to a tsetse-infested southern reserve. Many died on the long forced migration. During the ensuing half-century of colonial rule, the government pursued a policy aimed at restraining the warrior age-set, the core of Maasai conservatism. They saw the warriors as gangs of restless young men who planned raids and terrorized the countryside, and they attempted to shift authority into the hands of the elders who seemed more compliant. The warriors, or *il-murran*, resisted fiercely, rebelling against the forcible enrollment of children in school and recruitment of warriors for military service and road construction.[5] The British declared the southern reserve a "closed district," prohibited the selling of Maasai stock, and blocked access to Somalia where the Maasai went to improve their stock. As a result, the Maasai were effectively shut out of Kenya's colonial market economy and relegated to the margin of society. In Tanzania's Serengeti and surrounding countryside, the Maasai faced similar coercive regulations of first the German and, later, the British authorities.

Of all the truly beautiful Maasai regions, Serengeti is the image of Ndorror, the Promised Land. *Sirenket*, the Maasai name for Serengeti, means "the extended place."[6] It is a land of endless space, large tracts of unbroken savannah, and permanent water—a grazing feast fanning out from the feet of Oldoinyo le Nkai, the Mountain of God. At 9,650 feet, Lengai, as it is more commonly known, is the only surviving active volcano in East Africa. The Maasai god resides on Lengai and his voice speaks to them through the fire and ash in its belly. It was Lengai who, in one violent convulsion, warned Mbatian about the coming of the white man and his railroad, the "black snake." It is still Lengai who guides the Maasai towards an uncertain future.

Where Lengai is the conscience of the Maasai, Sirenket is the wellspring of their passion. With long, untiring legs, the Maasai found in the Serengeti the space they needed for walking and the sweet grasses and running water for herding. If the Serengeti has been their lifeblood, in a very real sense, too, the Serengeti has been sustained by the Maasai who have lived in intimate harmony with it.

From the earliest days of German rule in Tanganyika at the century's turn, however, there were other plans for the whole northern portion of Maasailand which included the Ngorongoro Crater Highlands and the Serengeti plains. Germany intended to confine the Maasai to a reserve on the arid Maasai steppe and put the Ngorongoro district and the Serengeti plains into large-scale agricultural and livestock production. This grandiose plan did not succeed but, as a measure of their tenacity, Ngorongoro Crater's floor was partitioned for farming and rich Maasai lands around Mount Kilimanjaro and Mount Meru were taken away. The transfer of power to the British after the First World War brought a reprieve until the late 1930s, when the Maasai again saw their lands distributed piecemeal for settler farms.

The Serengeti plains survived as a grazing preserve of the Maasai until 1959. Then, under extreme pressure from the colonial administration and international wildlife preservationists, the Maasai abandoned the plains and retreated to the newly demarcated conservation area. The promised compensatory water points proved drastically inadequate and, over time, many parts of the conservation area were closed to the Maasai, particularly the floor of Ngorongoro Crater, an excellent dry season pasture and salt lick. Fire, a traditional tool in pasture management, was prohibited, thereby allowing unpalatable grasses to flourish and further diminishing suitable graze.

In 1975, the policy of multiple land use, upon which the conservation area was founded, was altered with a ban on cultivation. Contrary to the popular image of an exclusively meat- and blood-eating people, the Maasai have always cultivated or traded for crops as a dry season supplement. The government's compensatory grain supplies to the Maasai village shops have not offset the shortages caused by the cultivation ban and, consequently, there is periodic hunger in Maasailand today.[7] Forced to sell stock to buy food, the Maasai are reducing both the reproductive capacity of their herds and their milk yields. They also appear to be increasing their herds of goats and sheep—the small change of a pastoral economy—at the expense of their cattle. The smaller stock will, eventually, degrade the land because of different grazing practices. The thirty years of conservation management in the Serengeti have placed the Maasai in a precarious position which has led to hunger, thirst, and tragedy. In 1980, a particularly bad season, the temptation to stray from his path was irresistible, and a Maasai warrior was shot dead as he brought his family's cattle to water in Olduvai Gorge. His crime was trespassing on the lands of his forefathers, which are no longer his own.[8]

Masek is an alkaline lake lying just outside the southern boundary of Serengeti National Park. Together with neighboring Lake Ndutu, they create an important water system which feeds into Olduvai Gorge. Even if one were unaware of the astounding excavations of paleontologist Mary Leakey, the flaked handtools found casually scattered along the river bed in the dry season tell a vivid story of man's long-standing dependency on these waters. The gorge and its feeder lakes and marshes are still vital to the survival of the Maasai and their herds. As May slips into June and June drags into July, the waters vanish from the gorge, leaving a dry, stony river bed. But a slightly salty seepage feeds the marshes of Masek year-round, and it is to this reedy, wet place that the Maasai bring their cattle when their wells have run dry. Along with fifteen thousand other head of cattle from all corners of Tanzania's Maasailand, Njilalo's Nasera herd will wait out the dry season here. In the cool of the early morning, droves of three-hundred or more cattle fan out along the length of the marsh and cautiously venture into the sticky, black mud to drink their fill. The air sings with the timbre of bells and lowing mingled with the sounds of chopping, song, and laughter.

The warriors, splendid in their beads, finely

braided hair embellished with silver ornaments, and ochred togas, seem inappropriately dressed for the work at hand, the construction of dams. Their arrogant mien and indolent stance—arm draped around another's shoulders—belies their interest, let alone their ability, in such mundane concerns. Yet they set to work chopping and splitting branches from the surrounding acacias and fashioning them into barriers. The style and tempo is pure Maasai, disorderly yet dynamic. A young elder, with longer toga and shaved head, oversees the construction with a switch that he cracks on the naked buttocks of a lazy youth. Met with peals of laughter and a light-hearted chase, the idler returns sheepishly to the job. A young woman, lovely in her beaded skirt and headdress, sings encouraging words, urging her cattle through the mire. The scene is ancient, biblical. The watering of cattle has not changed since the days of Abel.

A nomad's life—the need to protect his wealth on the hoof and his choice of a migration path—is conditioned by the vagaries of nature and the skill and risk-taking with which he meets them.[9] A man can be ruined in one season. Survival requires intimacy with the environment and flexibility. A shepherd must so completely identify with his surrounding landscape that it ceases to be a threatening wilderness and becomes, instead, a place of spiritual relevance.

The way in which the nomad possesses this land is to invest it with power, and this he does by naming it, telling stories about it, mythologizing it. Every place and feature of Serengeti-Mara has a name and often a story. Place-names are graphic, precise, and very informative. *Mara* ("dappled") implies shady trees just as *Sirenket* ("extended place") infers the lack of them.[10] The stories *enkatinyi* and *enkiterunoto*—those about history and those about beginnings—are the power and soul of Maasai culture, its affirmation. They are the connecting links between the Maasai individual and the universe, making sense of the inexplicable, providing the heroes, encapsulating life's lessons. They are also the direct line to the time and place of the ancestors. If a man does not know the stories, he cannot find the past and claim it as his own. A Maasai herdsman, using the stories and place-names as his key, reads his environment much as we read a map. What he is

also reading, however, is the cumulative experience of his ancestors who traveled the same pathways. To know his environment, therefore, is to know his culture's history and, ultimately, himself.

I spent many months camped in Maasailand during the 1970s. At the time, it seemed like a lifetime that would never end and my memories are vivid: the sweet smell of cattle; a midday walk across the plains accompanied by young warriors and the pride I felt at maintaining their pace; the endless drone of people's voices, as natural to my life as the cicadas' night song; and the lilting whistle of a young herd-boy driving his cattle across the river. Mostly, however, my images center around Njilalo, a senior elder about sixty years of age, who came from a town to the east where, he said, "only goats and sheep can live." He was an arrow and spear maker, and because I was camped in a stand of *ol sokonoi*, the wood he preferred for his craft, he decided to stay with me. Quiet and distant, with eyes that seemed to see into my soul, he whittled and filed away his days under the trees, enough apart to give him his peace but within earshot, if not sight, of all the comings and goings of camp life. One day he handed me a present—a beaded necklace—and he instructed me to call him *Papai* ("my father"). I thought he would be friendlier then, but instead he became more critical. He scolded me for spilling the milk, for letting the fire die out, for my poor progress with his language. Upset, more in embarrassment than anger, I began to make that extra effort which slowly changed our relationship.

One evening, as we sat around the warming coals, Papai told me, "If you want to learn about the Maasai, you must begin as a child." Every night thereafter, he would tell me of the Great Wars, teach me children's poems and songs, recount fantastic myths, recite prayers, or count, in the Maasai way, with a wiggle and flick of the fingers. His eyes that had once haunted me with their silent judgment became the windows through which I came to see his world.

My favorite time with Papai was spent on our "naming" walks, when he would take me out, spear in hand, and painstakingly identify the world that surrounded us. Different carving woods, medicinal plants, earths with magical properties—his was the knowledge of a man of the forest, and I began to suspect that Papai had some less than perfect pastoralist's blood in his veins. His knowledge extended to the landscape's features—outstanding like the solitary Euphorbia tree on the plain, or common-place, a rocky hilltop—and he had stories for them all. He called the wide and winding Mara River, which issues from the Mau Escarpment, *Enkapai*, from the Maasai word, *enkape*, meaning a cow's afterbirth. He said that, as with the afterbirth, if you rub this water on your forehead, it would make you always be kind to cattle. He named our wooded campsite *Encoruet* ("friend") and the name endured. To bless my home, he picked some grass underfoot and spat on it, then marked the trees with cinnamon-colored earth.

While my home was fast becoming fixed in the constellation of Maasai villages, there were others which were being uprooted. When the boundaries of the Mara Game Reserve were redesigned in the mid-1970s, many Maasai found themselves on the wrong side of the line. Expulsion, the burning of cattle *kraals*, and even fines for those Maasai found walking within park boundaries followed, and these incidences revealed to me the changing times and impending conflict. When I spoke to Papai about the troubling future, he would say, "The other side is dark"—you cannot see into the future.

When you take a nomad's land away, interrupting his migration path and destroying his spiritual and cultural landmarks, you are altering something so much more than a pastoralist's lifestyle. When you take a nomad's land away you are erasing his stories, the collective memory of his culture, the map he must give his children so that they can find their way back to themselves.

Alberto Moravia has said, "There is no greater suffering for man than to feel his cultural foundations giving way beneath his feet."[11] Papai knew that the ways of the Maasai were changing and, like elders in other cultures, he was saddened that many young Maasai did not respect their traditions. After all, he would say, "A zebra does not despise its own stripes." On the other hand he seemed to place a generous amount of faith in the continuity of life which he felt, like the cycles of plenty and dearth, proceeds in spite of man's meddling hand. I could not help feeling that his faith was misguided.

When I left Papai at the end of my stay, standing on an airstrip in the middle of the plains, he picked some grass, spat, and rubbed it on my forehead in blessing. "Papai," I said. "I will see you at *Encoruet* in five months time." He quietly responded, "You know where you are coming from but not where you are going. If it's God's will, we will meet by the river in the tenth month."

Papai died not long after I left. *Encoruet* has reverted to thick bush and even our carved names in the trunk of a fig tree are slowly disappearing under the encroaching bark. Nature is often remarkably resistent to intrusion. The years' passing and countless examples worldwide prove that cultures are not. The changes in Kenya's and Tanzania's Maasailand are profound and distressing and none are more crucial, more pivotal, than the loss of Maasai lands and, most importantly, their beloved Sirenket. Responding to these changes with a characteristic mix of pride, dignity, and disdain, an old man takes his grandson to the foot of Oldoinyo Lengai, the Mountain of God, and says:

> I am old my child, and many days have passed since the time when I wore the headdress of the black-mane lion. We have been forced by the Il Meek to leave our best lands; we no longer fight, for the Maasai say, 'Do not look for stolen cattle armed only with a herding stick . . .'
>
> Old men do not understand changes. My remaining days are few; the future is of little matter to me. I have lived in the manner of my father and his father. And shall I not die as they did?. . . . It is not for myself I fear. I say, I shall die as a Maasai, but I have no certainty for my children.
>
> I have brought you to this place that you might view the Mountain of God, that you might know the home of your father's father. And it is here where I shall tell you all the ways of the people of Maa, that you may never forget them whatever comes.

And the child responds, "My father, I hear."[12]

LISA LINDBLAD

1. The author uses the Maa-language spelling, it being the acceptable form of the Maasai people.

2. This historical summary follows that set out in Richard Lamprey and Richard Waller's chapter, "The Loita-Mara Area in Historical Times," in Peter Robertshaw's upcoming book, *Early Pastoralists of South-western Kenya*.

3. Århem, Kaj, "The Maasai and the State: The Impact of Rural Development Policies on a Pastoral People in Tanzania," *IWGIA Document* no. 52:33.

4. Baumann, Oscar, quoted in *A Modern History of Tanzania*, John Iliffe (Cambridge: Cambridge University Press, 1970), p. 124.

5. This period of Maasai history is discussed by Robert L. Tignor in "The Maasai Warriors: Pattern Maintenance and Violence in Colonial Kenya," in JAH, XIII, 2 (1972), pp. 271–290.

6. Parkipuny, L. M. S., "On Behalf of the People of Ngorongoro," background paper for the 1981 Management Plan of the Ngorongoro Conservation Area, 1981, p. 3.

7. For a complete discussion of the effects of socioeconomic changes on the diet of the Ngorongoro Maasai, see "A Pastoral Food System: The Ngorongoro Maasai of Tanzania," Århem, Kaj, Katherine Homewood, and Alan Rogers, Bureau of Resource Assessment and Land Use Planning, University of Dar Es Salaam, no. 70, 1981. Also Kaj Århem, *Pastoral Man in the Garden of Eden* (Uppsala: University of Uppsala, 1985).

8. Parkipuny, op. cit., p. 22.

9. Many of my observations, experiences and feelings recounted in these paragraphs were sharpened after reading Bruce Chatwin's remarkable book, *The Songlines*. It is rare to be able to project one's own experience against a backdrop as perfectly painted as I have been able to do with Chatwin's writings.

10. For a wonderful list of placename translations and explanations, see Fr. Frans Mol's *Maa: A Dictionary of the Maasai Language and Folklore* (Nairobi: Marketing & Publishing Ltd., 1979), pp. 121–124.

11. Moravia, Alberto, *Which Tribe Do You Belong To?* (St. Albans: Granada Publishing Ltd., 1976), p. 70.

12. Massek, A. ol'Oloisolo and J. O. Sidai, *Wisdom of Maasai* (Nairobi: Transafrica Publishers, 1974), p. 8.

Page 157: Warriors building dams at Masek

Pages 158–159: Young elder herding cattle

Pages 160–161: Maasai house

Page 161: Maasai village enclosure

Pages 162–163: Warriors on the plains   161

Page 164: Warriors' decoration

Page 165: Old women greeting

Pages 166–167: Rock paintings depicting Maasai shield designs at Moru Kopjes

Page 168: Laibon Ole Sentue Simel, grandson of Mbatian

Page 169 (above left): Maasai warriors

Page 169 (above right): Mother shaving her warrior son's head during a Eunoto ceremony

Page 169 (below left): Girls in a village

Page 169 (below right): Warriors with shaved heads at a Eunoto ceremony's conclusion

Pages 170–171: Crater of Oldoinyo Lengai, the Mountain of God

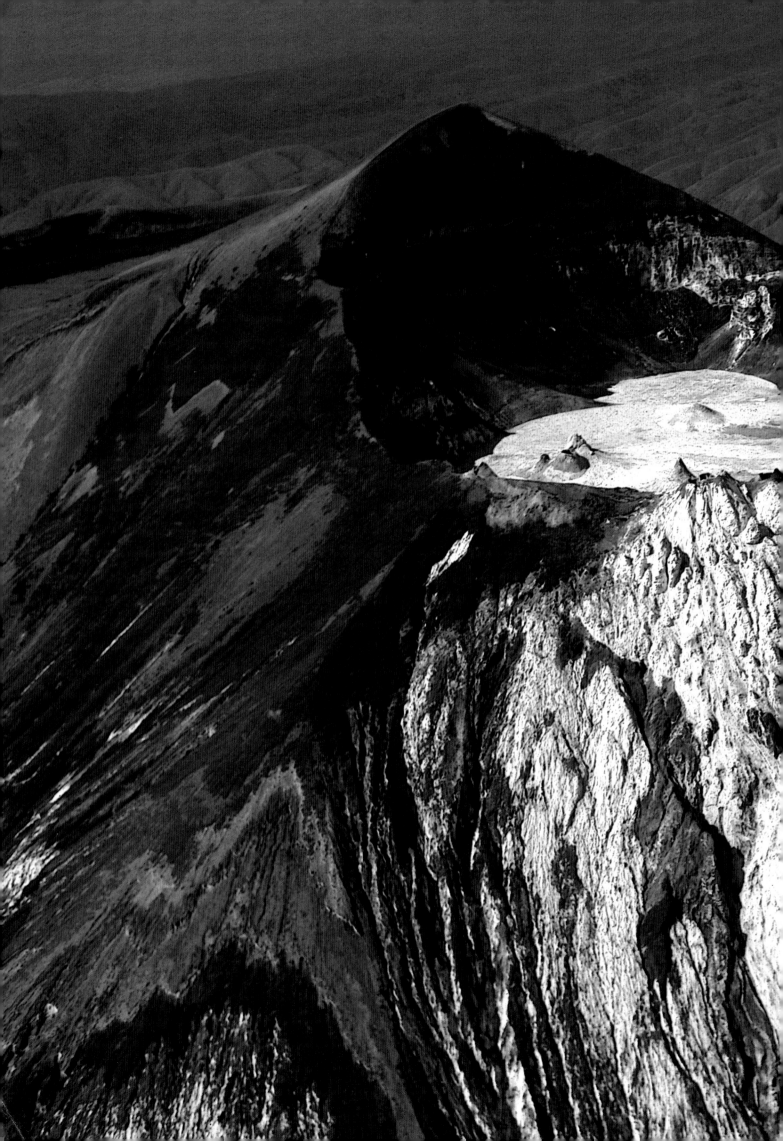

Pages 172–173: Boy with cattle at Empakai

Page 174: Newly circumcised boy's headdress made of stuffed birds

SELECT BIBLIOGRAPHY

Amin, M., D. Willets, and J. Eames. *The Last of the Maasai*, London: The Bodley Head, 1987.

Arhem, Kaj. *Pastoral Man in the Garden of Eden: The Maasai of the Ngorongoro Conservation Area, Tanzania*, Uppsala: University of Uppsala, 1985.

Bower, J. R. F. & P. Gogan-Porter. *Prehistoric Cultures of the Serengeti National Park*, Iowa: Iowa State University Press, 1981.

Grzimek, B. and M. Grzimek. *Serengeti Shall Not Die*, London: Hamish Hamilton, 1960.

Hay, R. L. *Geology of the Olduvai Gorge*, Los Angeles: University of California Press, 1976.

Hayes, H. T. P. *The Last Place on Earth*, New York: Stein and Day, 1977.

Kessel, J. *Le Lion*, Paris: Gallimard, 1958.

Leakey, M. D. *Laetoli: A Pliocene Site in Northern Tanzania*, Oxford: Oxford University Press, 1987.

———. *Olduvai Gorge, Volume 3*, Cambridge: Cambridge University Press, 1979.

Massek, A. ol'Oloisolo and J. O. Sidai. *Wisdom of Maasai*, Nairobi: Transafrica Publishers, 1974.

Matthiessen, P. and E. Porter. *The Tree Where Man Was Born*, New York: E. P. Dutton & Co., 1972.

Mol, F. Fr. *Maa: A Dictionary of the Maasai Language and Folklore*, Nairobi: Marketing & Publishing Ltd., 1978.

Moravia, A. *Which Tribe Do You Belong To?* St. Albans: Granada Publishing Company, 1976.

New York Zoological Society. *Animal Kingdom: The Zoological Society Magazine*, no. 3, vol. 87.

Phillipson, D. W. *African Archaeology*, Cambridge: Cambridge University Press, 1984.

Read, D. *Barefoot Over the Serengeti*, Nairobi: The Travel Book Club, 1979.

Read, D. and P. Chapman. *Waters of the Sanjan*, Nairobi: David William Lister Read, 1982.

Reader, J. *Missing Links*, London: Collins, 1981.

Saitoti, T. ole. *The Worlds of a Maasai Warrior: An Autobiography*, New York: Random House, 1986.

Saitoti, T. ole and C. Beckwith. *Maasai*, New York: Harry N. Abrams, 1980.

Sankan, S. S. ole. *The Maasai*, Nairobi: East African Literature Bureau, 1971.

Schaller, G. B. *Serengeti: A Kingdom of Predators*, New York: Alfred A. Knopf, 1972.

———. *Serengeti Lion: A Study of Predator-Prey Relations*, Chicago: Chicago University Press, 1972.

Sinclair, A. R. E. & M. Norton-Griffiths. *Serengeti: Dynamics of an Ecosystem*, Chicago: University of Chicago Press.

Sorrenson, M. P. K. *Origins of European Settlement in Kenya*, Nairobi: Oxford University Press, 1968.

Turner, M., edited by Brian Jackman. *My Serengeti Years*, London: Hamish Hamilton, 1987.

Vesey-Fitzgerald, D. *East African Grasslands*, Nairobi: East African Publishing House, 1973.

ABOUT THE CONTRIBUTORS

George B. Schaller is a field biologist with Wildlife Conservation International, a division of the New York Zoological Society. Specializing in the research and conservation of large mammals, he has studied gorillas, tigers, lions, and jaguars. His work in recent years has largely been devoted to China, studying the giant panda and the unique wildlife of the Plateau of Tibet.

Allan Earnshaw, who has been leading safaris in East Africa since 1970, is currently the chairman of Ker & Downey Kenya Ltd., Kenya's oldest safari company. A fourth-generation Kenyan, he was educated at Oxford University where he pursued his interests in animal behavior, ecology, and anthropology. Earnshaw provided the anthropological research on the nomadic tribes living around Lake Turkana for *Cradle of Mankind.*

Sandy Price, from 1969 until 1987, lived in Kenya, where she was involved in a number of projects. These included the Wildlife Clubs of Kenya Association, which she developed and administered for nine years, and the African Wildlife Foundation where she held the position of Director of African Operations. Upon her return to the United States, Ms. Price worked for Wildlife Conservation International in New York, preparing exhibitions and public outreach programs. She now resides in California.

Keith Shackleton's passionate interest in wildlife has always been expressed in his painting. Currently Chairman of the Artists League of Great Britain, he has traveled the world over and has been part of many expeditions. He has worked as a naturalist aboard the M.S. *Lindblad Explorer,* mainly in Antarctica and the Pacific islands, and has traveled extensively through Africa, the Andes, and The Himalayas. Since 1979 Shackleton has presented in Great Britain a children's wildlife program, "Animals in Action," which has an international audience.

Sven-Olof Lindblad is a trustee of the African Wildlife Foundation, Washington, D.C., and President of Special Expeditions, the highly successful New York-based firm he founded in 1979 which specializes in adventure travel. He lived six years in Kenya and Tanzania, photographing elephants in Tsavo National Park, managing a tented camp, and working on films—notably a World Wildlife Fund documentary on the impact of forest destruction on East Africa. His photographs have appeared in *National Geographic, Smithsonian, International Wildlife, Signature,* and various Audubon books.

Lisa Lindblad is the co-author with her husband, Sven, of *Alaska: Southeast to McKinley* and *Baja California.* Her involvement with Africa dates back to 1971 when she drove overland from London to Kenya. In the mid-1970s, she lived for over a year among the Masai in the Masai Mara. Ms. Lindblad received her graduate degrees in social anthropology from Columbia University. She frequently returns to Africa with Sven and their two sons, Justin and Jeremy.

PHOTOGRAPH CREDITS

All photographs by Sven-Olof Lindblad except:
Shep Abbott: 148–149
Alan Binks: 8–9, 20–21, 40–41, 52–53, 56–57, 95
Aadje Geertsma: 82 (below)
Nigel R. Pavitt: 36–37, 74–75, 85, 152–153, 160–161, 165, 168, 169, 174
George B. Schaller: 70–71
Jonathan Scott: 17, 83, 89, 90–91, 92, 93, 96 (below), 118–119, 122, 123, 130, 141